Dedication

To my only child, Cheri, who shares my love of pets and animals. She has somehow managed to bring many lost and orphaned animals into my life, all of which have been great blessings that have helped me through many trying times. Thank God for Cheri and my pets.

Joy Johns

To order additional copies of this book, contact:
Xlibris
844-714-8691
www.Xlibris.com
Orders@Xlibris.com

ISBN: Softcover   978-1-4415-4051-5
        EBook   978-1-6641-4785-0

Print information available on the last page

Rev. date: 12/10/2020

Pig Tales

Written by

Joy Johns

And narrated by

Porkchop

BEGINNINGS

Let's see. . . How should I begin these tales? *Once upon a time, there were TWO little pigs.* . . Nah, that's been done. How about, *Here comes trouble*? Nope, that's over done. I got it! *I am a pig....and proud of it!*

Did you know that we pigs are one of the smartest creatures in the animal kingdom? And, we are one of the most popular characters in tales, books, movies, and cartoons. Think about it. There's the famous Three Little Pigs, Babe, Gordy, Arnold, Porky, Piglet, Wilbur, Hamm, Ms. Piggy and countless others. However, there are not many piggy autobiographies. So, I pick this form to tell my story, illustrated with pages from my very own photo album.

TALE 1

Way Down Upon the Suwannee River

They call me Porkchop, *they* being those mixed up creatures called humans. I live with one of these troubled creatures, and with my big step-brother Oink. Also sharing our abode are two noisy parrots and an old dog. Our keeper is a lonely old lady. She is fat, homely and grouchy, but we love her *almost* more than food, and that's saying a lot coming from a pig! Her name is Ms. Joy, but we call her *Mom.*

The birds and dog came first. The red and green parrots are called S.B. and B.B. I don't know why, but I can guess. Could one be *Stupid Bird* and the other *Busy Bird*? The aged terrier is black, so *Pepper* is a good name. They lived with Mom many years before her divorce, after which she decided to move to North Florida. This is where her daughter, Cheri, lives. Mom found a five acre homestead close to a small town on the famous Suwannee River. She and the parrots often sang, "*Way down upon the Suwannee River, that's where I roam... Way down upon the Suwannee River, that's where I call my home.*" Here, Mom and her pets looked forward to a new beginning. They loved the peace and beauty of the pastoral lands surrounding their little homestead. There was harmony in this new household. Everybody shared and took turns. S.B. and B.B. sang songs to Mom and shared snacks, frequently calling "Oh, Joy--Oh, Joy!" They gave her loving pecks and playful nips. Pepper was always sweet and shy, seeking hugs and sneaking kisses, always ready to share. In this household, sharing was love.

Despite all this affection and good will, Mom was still sad, bored and lonely. Although she liked being the boss and being in charge of things, something was missing, but she couldn't quite put her finger on it. Maybe life was just too predictable down here on the Suwannee River. Yes, that's it, Mom was bored. However, all this was about to change.

Sharing is LOVE

TALE 2

Moving In and Out

Let's begin with my older step-brother. He was rescued by Mom's daughter, Cheri. She bought him for $5 at an auction, a low bid because he was a cross between a regular farm hog and a pot-belly pig. Everyone there thought this half-breed was worthless. He was all black and so little he could fit in a baseball cap. Cheri put him in the back seat of her car. By the time she walked back around the car to get into the driver's seat, he was sitting in the front passenger's seat. On the way home he jumped back and forth between the front and back seat and squealed so loud that Cheri's ears hurt. He flew around the car as though he had wings! But by the time they pulled into her driveway, she was in love. And, as the days passed, he fell in love with Cheri.

She named him Oink because he wouldn't shut up, grunting with every step. He made dozens of sounds when trying to talk to his beloved keeper, sometimes giggling, sighing, laughing or crying. She swore he was sometimes trying to say *Mama*! But the rest of the family only heard *Oink Oink*.

He especially enjoyed talking to shoes. Any kind of shoes would start Oink chatting...sneakers, boots, flip-flops, slippers. He adored shoes, whether occupied by a foot or not. To this day, Oink loves to engage in *shoe-talk*, but if presented with a barefoot, he grunts with loud displeasure, maybe even nipping a toe!

Well, as the weeks passed, their affection grew for one another. Cheri soon began letting Oink inside the house, where they played for hours. He loved to lie down in front of the fireplace. He also liked to stretch out next to her for a belly rub. Oink would rather have a rub than a treat! Sometimes she would sneak him into bed with her. Oink would lie very still all night long, nestled in her arms.

However, as Oink grew, his welcome lessened. In less than a year he approached 200 pounds. Cheri's husband and three kids thought that he was fat, mean and ugly, but she thought he was quite handsome. Her family also turned against this huge, black hog because he became quite possessive and jealous. Cheri was the light of his life. All others had to beware, or he would nip and butt them if they came near his cherished caregiver. So, much to Cheri's displeasure, he was banned from the house and booted into the small, fenced yard. Here there were no trees, no bed, and no fireplace—such a *bummer*!

Oink soon began to root, something that pigs do with their snouts, digging up holes in the ground. Sometimes we root for food, like roots and acorns, sometimes to make beds for wallowing or sunning, and sometimes just to play. In no time Oink was rooting up the whole back yard! Much to Cheri's dismay, the rest of the family declared that this monstrous hog had to go!

She searched and searched for a new home for her beloved pet, but no one wanted such a huge, overbearing creature. Besides, he was now sporting sharp and scary tusks. Even the mailman, meter readers and visitors were frightened of him and refused to enter the yard. Cheri told everyone that Oink wouldn't hurt a flea, but no one believed her.

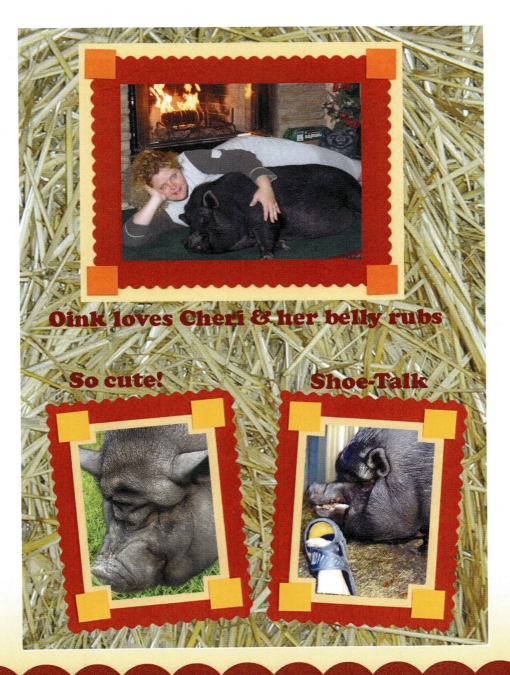

Oink loves Cheri & her belly rubs

So cute!   Shoe-Talk

Rooting...

Not so cute anymore!

TALE 3

Pigs Rule!

In desperation, Cheri talked Mom into adopting Oink. Mom had plenty of room on her 5 acre homestead, but she wanted to protect Oink from all the wild coyotes and bobcats which roamed this rural area. Also, she wanted to protect her 5 acres from pig rooting. So, she proceeded to build a pen in the backyard. She even bought him an expensive dog house shaped like an igloo to protect him from the cold winter nights in North Florida. Well, Oink would have none of this nonsense!

It was a cold January night when he arrived. Mom put him into the back pen and went to bed, but she couldn't sleep. Visions of wild animals attacking her new guest made her uneasy. Besides, he would be cold if he didn't take to his new house. So, at midnight she crawled out of bed and went out into the chilly darkness to check on him. Oink was no where to be seen! She called and called. Then she saw what had happened. Oink had overturned the igloo and had torn down the fence.

It was freezing cold, but Mom wandered all over her property in nothing but her nightgown, calling and searching for Oink. Thank goodness there was a full moon. Then she spied him out by the front gate. But when she came near, he ran. She tried and tried to coax him into the back pen where he'd be warm and safe, but Oink would have none of that. The closer she came, the faster he ran. So there they were on that cold January night, running around and around in the moonlight—a sight to behold. Finally, after losing her voice from screaming, Mom gave up and went back to bed.

The next morning she found Oink, safe and sound, under the front porch. Mom decided, much to Oink's delight, to let him roam free all over the homestead, and to let him root and dig to his heart's content. After all, even if this guest only survived a short while, he would be much happier roaming free than confined in a pen. She made him a warm and safe house under the front porch, which was the spot that Oink had chosen for his home. He hated that igloo—after all, he was no Eskimo!

Oink wandered all over the property, rooting to his heart's content! He grazed freely on the lush grasses and tasty acorns under the oak tress. Mom even added a concrete patio on the front of his house to protect the entrance and to give him a nice area for eating and drinking. This was heaven, where pigs rule! In fact, she decided that *PIG HEAVEN* would make a good name for her little farm.

As the months passed, Oink's love for Mom grew, but he never forgot Cheri. When he heard her car approaching, he'd waddle up to the gate to meet her. Then he would insist that she lie down in the yard and give him a belly rub before going inside! Yes, indeed, pigs rule!

As spring turned into summer and summer into fall, Mom began to worry that Oink might be lonely. The two parrots were terrified of him, and Pepper was totally indifferent. Mom tried to pay him lots of attention. She let him in every morning to have breakfast with her. No matter that this huge hog took up almost half of her living room. Mom enjoyed his company, especially when he would lie down in front of her fireplace next to Pepper, while she sipped her morning coffee and read the newspaper.

In the afternoons, they would lounge on the front porch and listen to the singing of the wind and the wild birds. Sometimes Oink would strike up a conversation with Mom's shoe, making her giggle. But if she didn't have a treat ready when he wanted one, he would butt her with his snout. Or, when she decided to put him back outside, he would try to push her over backwards, while squealing in high pitched protests. In spite of these antics, Oink seemed to enjoy his sojourn in Pig Heaven. However, his keeper still worried that he might need a fellow pig for a companion.

Oink's new house & patio

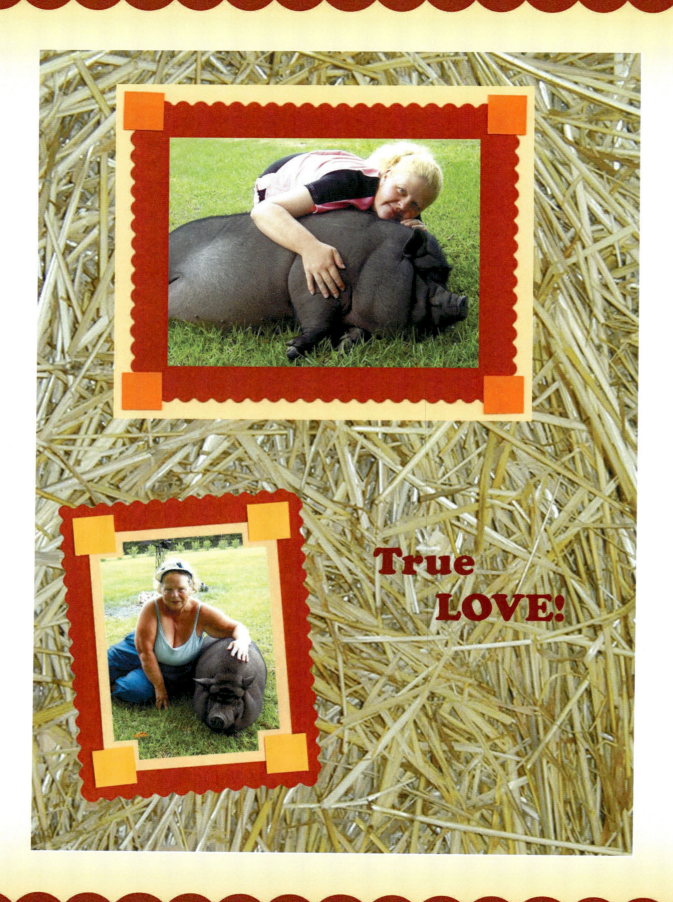

True
LOVE!

TALE 4

The Newcomer

One day Mom went shopping at a local flea market. There, she came upon a sight to behold. A man was selling baby pigs. They were miniature pot bellies, and he guaranteed that they would stay small due to their breeding. She fell in love with a grey one, all dotted with black spots and patches, with a pink belly. She wrapped him in a blanket and took him home. She could have named him Patches or Spot....But no, she called me *Porkchop*!

Mom couldn't wait to introduce me to Oink. But, what she didn't know is that pigs are not social beings. We like our independence and want to be the head honcho , the boss. We don't relish competition. Oink was always telling Mom what to do and wanted all her affection for himself alone. So, when I arrived on Oink's doorstep, he rebelled, howling with resentment. Of course I squealed in terror. He charged and threatened, making me run to Mom to be rescued. "Oh my, What have I done?" Mom wondered. She had to watch us very closely for the first several weeks, as Oink meant business. Although I could outmaneuver this lumbering giant, Mom didn't want to take a chance.

Not long after my arrival, Cheri came over to meet Oink's new Brother. She couldn't believe how sweet and cute I was, so she was dismayed by Oink's rejection. However, he was just being a pig and doing what pigs do. He was quite jealous and feeling rejected. And, he was protecting his position as head-pig! Later that day Cheri decided to lie down on the floor and take a nap, but I wanted to play. So, I crawled up onto her back and tried to wake her up. When this didn't work, I decided to take a nap with her, finding a perfect spot between her legs. Her butt made a comfy pillow, and Mom, thinking this would make a great photo, scurried to find the camera.

Because of my small size, Mom let me stay inside until I grew larger. She gave me a bed in the family room, but at night I slept in her closet, not wanting to be far from her protective eye. Every morning I woke up at exactly 5 AM, no alarm clock necessary. Then I went over to her bedside and grunted softly until she woke up and let me outside into the back pen she had built for Oink, where I could eat breakfast and be safe from my big brother's aggression. We followed this routine for several months, till I was big enough to live safely outside. Mom built me a house next to the front porch door, right on top of Oink's abode—making a piggy condominium!

Cheri meets Oink's
new brother...

Too little to sleep outside...

Too big to sleep inside!

TALE 5

Growing Up

As the months passed, I quickly increased in size. Mom was amazed by how fast I was growing. In fact, I was soon almost half as big as Oink, much bigger than the flea market merchant had predicted! I was always hungry and ate "like a PIG!" In fact, I gobbled down much more than my big brother. I relished the acorns that fell from dozens of Oak trees on our property, which were very fattening. To this day, I would rather have a cookie than a belly rub, but not Oink!

My big brother gradually accepted me into the family. However, his house and his food dish are still off limits to me. This I don't understand because he permits the neighborhood cats to enter his house and eat out of his dish. Even the wild crows are welcomed to his patio. As soon as Oink finishes his meals, they swoop down and clean up all the crumbs. He even permits them to sit on his dish. However, If I come anywhere near his patio, he charges and chases me away. He also insists on being a bully when we are both inside, so Mom usually lets us inside one at a time. Otherwise she has to play referee.

Oink and I enjoy being outside together. We roam the grounds, rooting and digging and playing in the giant holes we make. Oink has given me many rooting lessons, and now I am a better rooter than he is! Mom's yard looks like a bomb site, but she doesn't seem to mind, as now she has less grass to cut.

We always look forward to days when Mom comes out to burn trash. She has a big burn hole, which she has fenced to keep us out. There is a yard swing next to this area, so she can sit and watch the fire. On trash burning days, we follow her out to the site, hoping she will drop a morsel or two for us to sample as she tosses the bags over into the fire. When she sits down in the swing, we always stretch out by her feet, hoping for a belly rub. We all three enjoy watching the fire as the crackling embers float upwards into the surrounding trees.

Mom lets us inside to visit quite often because both of us are housebroken. We would never think of soiling our houses, outside or inside. We don't have fleas or ticks, and we don't bark or cry—well, not often, anyway. And, we are such good company. Our lonely old keeper welcomes our pig chatter and loves it when we flop down on her feet, getting as close as possible. Also, we are very clean, except when we decide to take a dip in one of our mud holes. Then Mom has to hose us down before we are allowed to visit inside. But, we don't mind, as this is a great game.

Since we love to play in the mud so much, Mom built us our very own small pond below her goldfish pool. Fresh water always runs into the fish pool, which drains down into our pond, so we always have clean water. This is my favorite hangout, especially when I need time to myself—as most adolescents do! And I have a feeling that this is also one of Mom's favorite spots, as she seems to enjoy watching the goldfish and listening to the running water as it trickles out of the old pump and streams down small water falls into our pond. After all, the sound of running water is so relaxing. What a life here in Pig Heaven, where *pigs rule!*

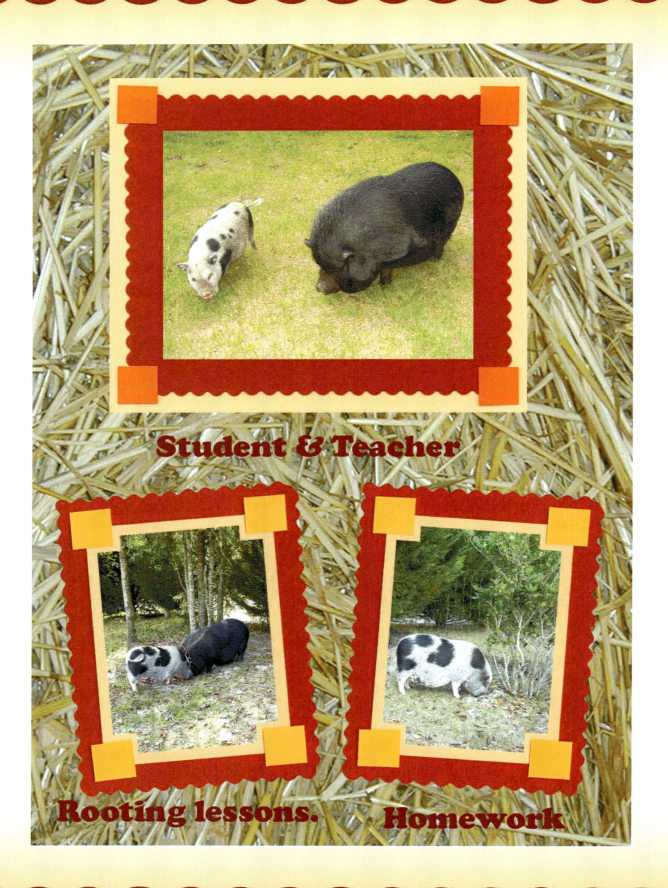

Student & Teacher

Rooting lessons.   Homework

Our favorite hangout

TALE 6

Fun and Games

Life is good down here on the Suwannee, where pigs rule, but Oink and myself both know that Mom is still having a hard time. She often sighs sadly and sheds a tear or two, so we both try to cheer her up. Oink still chatters a mile a minute, often gargling out his raspy "Mama", but I just grunt softly and nuzzle her hand.

Our favorite way to keep Mom from being lonely and bored is to make her laugh. We play many piggy games, including ball. We have a giant beach ball that we push all over the yard. Also we each have a plastic treat ball, which Mom fills with small treats. We move these around with our nose, making all the goodies fall out on the ground.

I like to play *tag*, especially when Mom rides her electric scooter. She chases me and honks the horn, and I run away—sometimes barking like a dog! Then, I turn suddenly and chase her. Around and around we go, Mom laughing so hard that she almost falls off the scooter.

Oink's favorite game is playing with plastic bags. He shakes them and twists them and tears them up into shreds, making a mess for Mom to clean up, but she smiles anyway. I like to stick my head into empty boxes and wear them on my head like a clown, making her giggle.

We both enjoy moving around Mom's yard ornaments, thinking that fixing them back will surely give her something fun to do. We especially enjoy attacking all the concrete critters which Mom has carefully placed around the yard. My favorite is the fisher boy who sits on the bank of our pond. I love to push him down into the water. He usually goes for a swim several times a day! Oink's favorite is a trio of dogs, which he knocks over as soon as he discovers that Mom has set them back up. Such a fun game! .

Another game I enjoy is *hide and seek*. Sometimes Mom is frightened because she can't find me. One day she looked and looked and called and called, searching under the porch, behind the bushes and all the places where I usually hid. She was about to call Cheri for help, when she spied me under my bed cushion, which I had managed to pull over me. She smiled with relief.

Another fun game is moving things I find on the floor, especially Mom's clothes. Undies, bras, socks, pants, night gowns, sweat suits and anything I can drag with my snout or rake with my hooves ends up in my closet nest. After all, the bigger the nest, the better I sleep. If Mom is missing something, she knows where to look, which always makes her smile. However, one day this ritual got slightly out of hand, when I managed to get all tangled up in one of her bright red bikini tops, designed for plus sized ladies. Out I ran with this outrageous costume wrapped over my head and around my legs. I ran around the house, squealing in panic as I tripped over the rugs and spun around in circles. When Mom saw me, she laughed and grabbed the camera.

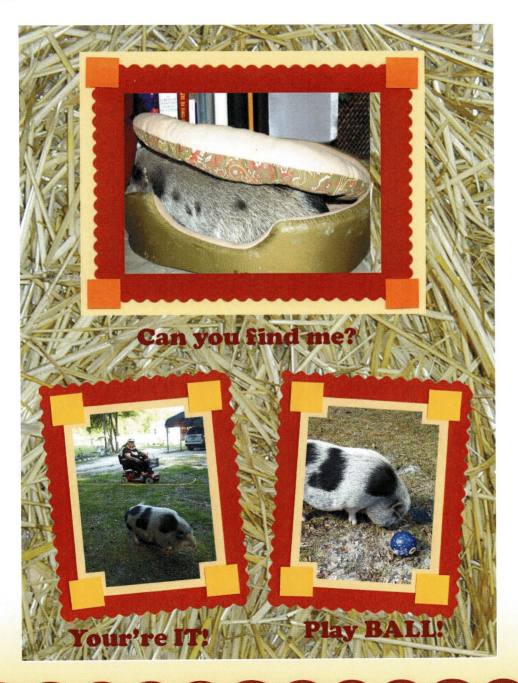

Can you find me?

Your're IT!

Play BALL!

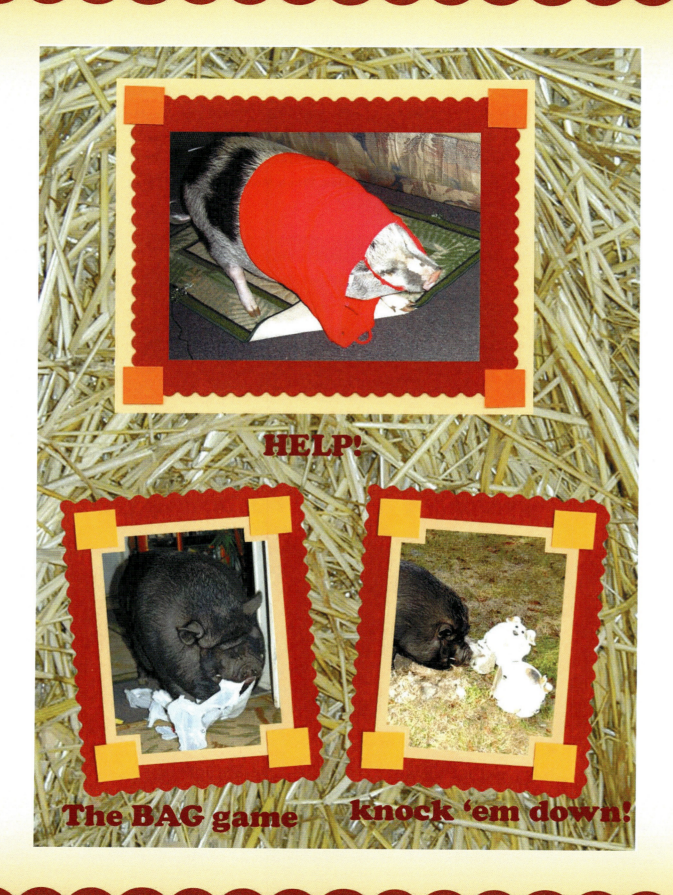

HELP!

The BAG game

knock 'em down!

Fisherman is going for a swim!

TALE 7

Juvenile Delinquents

Not all of our pig antics make Mom smile. For example, I love to chew on wires. Not long after my move into Pig Heaven, I discovered the many wires leading from the sound system all around the room. Well, these looked like fun to chew. Soon, the system didn't work. When Mom found the problem, she was furious. She repaired the wires, but in a short time found them all mangled again. After more tries, she decided to buy a new *wireless* system. Well, this problem was solved, but I quickly went looking for more wires to play with. I found the telephone cables and chewed away. Mom yelled in dismay, but I just cocked my head with that "Who me?" look. She was tired of having to watch me every minute. However, she didn't want to ban me from coming inside, as I was usually such good company. So, she went to the hardware store and purchased dozens of sections of metal shelving. She worked for many hours lining the rooms with shelving to prevent me from getting close to all the wires. Now the inside of the house looks like a jail!

She also had to put a section of this shelving across the door to the bird's room, as I often would sneak in there to sample all the bits of tasty goodies that B.B. and S.B. had thrown out on the floor. This was fine with Mom, as it kept her from having to vacuum so often. But, then I discovered that I could retrieve many more goodies by pulling out the newspaper from inside the cage bottom. After finding paper, bird food and droppings all over the floor, Mom banned me from going inside this room. Oh well, at least I could still come inside and visit. I had learned not only to open the porch door to let myself in, but how to open it from the inside when I chose to go back out. Pigs can work their snouts to open all kinds of doors, including pantries, refrigerators, closets and even drawers. So, Mom has to lock whatever doors she doesn't want opened.

So far, Oink opens the porch door to come in, but has not learned how to let himself back out. In fact, it is usually myself who gets into all the trouble inside. Oink just wants affection and is content to lie down close to Mom. He stays put until she orders him back outside, whereupon he cries like a baby and sometimes tires to bite or butt. Then Mom gets the broom. This is a time when pigs don't rule!

We also love to chew up cushions and papers, especially our bedding materials. After Mom spends hours lining our beds with pillows and blankets, we chew them up into hundreds of pieces and make a messy nest to our own liking. This makes Mom frown, especially when Oink rips up the pillow stuffing and scatters it all over the front yard! At least I keep mine in a neat nest. However, I know better than to tear up her good clothes that I find on the floor. However, Oink and I both love to drag around and rip apart Mom's good throw rugs. We know this really upsets her, but it's so much fun! No wonder she calls us juvenile delinquents.

Another one of our pig behaviors which makes Mom frown is our spoiled attitudes about treats. Whenever we obey her commands, she gives us a cookie, but now we are spoiled rotten, so much so that Mom has to bribe us with a treat before we will obey. She is especially frustrated by our refusal to go back outside until she hands us a treat. Then she yells, "Get out of here you juvenile delinquents!"

Perhaps we are at our worst when Mom ignores us! Then we resort to several stunts. If she is working on her lap top, I go over and try to chew on the wires. When she is talking on the phone, both of us knock over tables to make things fall on the floor. When Mom reads or naps in her recliner, we go over and butt the foot rest, almost tipping over her chair. Oink's favorite ploy to get attention is to attack the swivel rocker, spinning it around and around and around, until Mom stops whatever she is doing . He is sure to get noticed this way.

What is most irritating is our yard demolition. Although Mom tolerates our rooting, she flips out when we make a salad out of her favorite plants. My favorites are her lilies. Oink often devours her rose bushes, thorns and all! However, no matter how naughty we are, Mom always forgives us, and I am sure behind each angry frown is a great big smile.

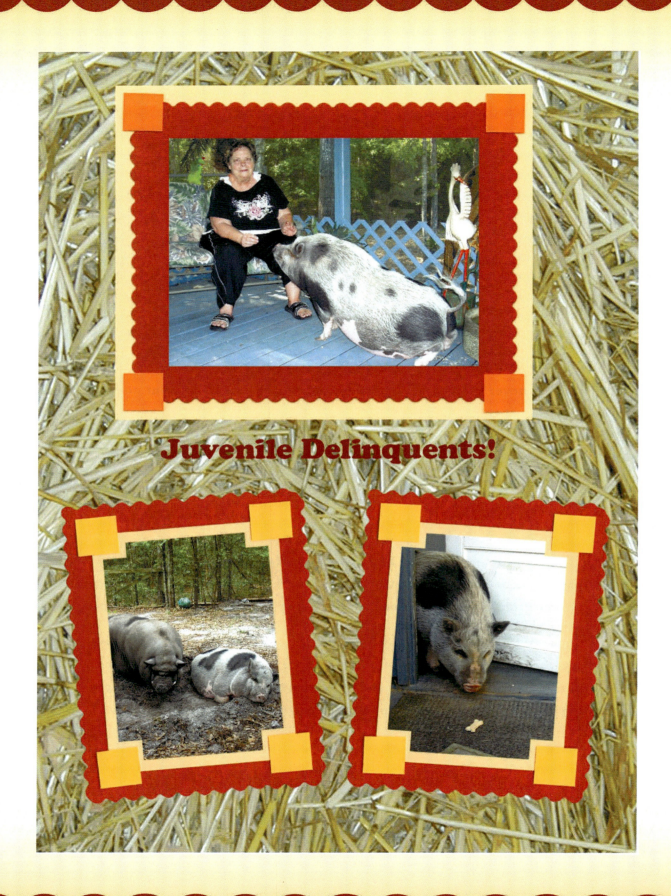

Juvenile Delinquents!

TALE 8

The Hose Caper

Sometimes there were some mysterious happenings on our little homestead, even a bit frightening. One day Mom went out to start her car to go shopping, but she noticed something was not quite right. Glancing around the yard, she noticed the water hose, all one hundred and fifty feet of it, had been stretched out into a straight line, all the way across the field. "Who or what did this?" she mused.

Oink loves her to squirt him and fill his holes with water so he can play in the mud, so he always follows her out to water the bushes. Not me, I like to play in the mud, but I don't like to be sprayed with the hose!

However, she always put the hose back into a neat coil in one special place near the driveway. Today she found it all pulled out into a line so tight that all the hose fittings were torn loose or broken. In fact, the hose was almost ripped off of the water faucet! Nevertheless, there were no tracks or footprints to be seen. "What on earth could have done this?" she asked herself again.

She was so upset by this strange event that she went back inside and called her daughter to see if she would have any answers. Cheri guessed that Oink may have done it, perhaps trying to invent a new piggy game, but Mom couldn't imagine him having the strength or ingenuity to pull off such a stunt. Besides, surely she would see some pig prints. So she fantasized that maybe *Bigfoot,* or a ghost or some other mythical creature living in the surrounding woods was behind this mysterious act. After all, those thick, dark woods next to our property are quite spooky, and sometimes we hear eerie sounds coming from back there.

To be truthful, I don't know the answer. Did Oink get bored and play tug-of-war with the hose? Or, was he trying to make the water run so he could take a mud bath? To this day he has never fessed up to this deed, but whenever it's brought up, he winks and smiles with glee. On the other hand, I am wondering why I am never considered a suspect, since I spend lots of time rooting and playing with the coiled up hose. I suppose I am just too cute to be a criminal.

To solve this troubling mystery once and for all, Mom asked Cheri to come over to investigate, but we pigs both pleaded innocent. Cheri couldn't imagine a person being behind this prank, as our homestead is fenced and gated. Besides, no one ever comes upon our property unless invited. So, Cheri was just as mystified as Mom, who still thinks that this infamous hose caper was carried out by some mysterious creature living back in the forest. Anyway, she sure is glad to have a *watch-pig* on duty!

Mom waters the bushes....
and Oink!

Who did it?   Not ME!!!!

Cheri questions the suspects

Guard Duty

TALE 9

Range Wars

Oink and myself have created troubles for Mom which extend beyond the fences of our pig heaven. The next door neighbors have two horses, which were terrified of us. As soon as they spied us out in the field, they would neigh in terror and stampede round and round their pasture. This infuriated their owners and caused bad feelings between them and Mom. Sometimes, when we pigs became bored, or when Mom was not home, we would go out to the fence and oink at the horses. What fun it was to see them kick their heels and run to hide behind their barn. It wasn't long before the neighbors had a talk with Mom, hinting that she was crazy for keeping such unworthy, pesky creatures as pigs and that perhaps she would be smart to get rid of us! Well, needless to say, Mom hasn't spoken to them since, and we spend more time than ever over by the fence where the horses can see us!

This was not the end of these unpleasant doings. These same neighbors also have several dogs, five Siberian Huskies. They are quite handsome, and strut by our fence in contempt. Huskies seldom bark, but these five howl and growl and show their teeth at us. We just are not popular with any of the creatures living next door.

A few weeks ago, the inevitable happened. It was a beautiful day, so Mom decided to go shopping, leaving Oink and me out in the yard. Well, these unruly dogs decided to go beyond growls. They managed to dig under the fence— all *five* of them! Immediately they started chasing us. Luckily, I am quick as greased lightening and outran them and let myself onto the screened-in front porch. But, they easily caught up to poor, old Oink—who was so fat and out of shape he could barely hobble. All of them cornered him and jumped on top of him. They proceeded to bite and claw him. He squealed in terror. Just in time, Mom drove up. She heard Oink's cries of pain and ran around to the back yard. When she saw what was happening, she grabbed the water hose and turned it on full force upon the frenzied, attacking dogs, who had pinned the helpless hog to the ground. All five dogs scattered when they felt the stream of cold water, and Mom chased them back under the fence. Then she rushed back to Oink.

He was hurt so badly that he couldn't even stand back up. His skin had been ripped open in dozens of places. As Mom dashed inside to call for help, she saw me hiding behind a chair on the front porch. She was so happy I had escaped the attack. She called a vet to come over to help Oink, as he was too big to lift or carry. The vet soon arrived, and much to Mom's relief, he reported that my big brother would be fine. Since a pig's skin is so tough, the bites were not deep, and the bleeding soon stopped. He left some antibiotics, and cautioned Mom to make sure that these dogs never got back into our yard again. Next time we might not be so lucky!

After the vet left, Mom called the neighbors to tell them what their dogs had done. They offered no help, and said that it was our problem, since dogs will be dogs, and pigs should not be roaming around, but kept in a pen where they belong!!! Well, Mom was afraid to leave or go anywhere, fearing that these mean dogs would get back under the fence. She had trouble sleeping at night, waking at every sound, fearing that the dogs might dig back in and attack again.

After many fearful days and sleepless nights, our mom went to see a lawyer, who wrote the neighbors a long letter, threatening a lawsuit. It worked. They soon installed an electric fence to insure that their dogs would never dig beneath our fence again. They even paid the vet's bill. Nevertheless, they have never spoken another word to Mom.

Oink and myself continue to parade up and down along our fence, trying to stir up some fun. The dogs are no longer allowed into the pasture which borders our fence, so we don't see them any more. However, the horses are getting used to us. In fact, they recently came over to the fence to introduce themselves and we have been telling them some of our pig tales. They seem to enjoy these chats, as they whinny and show their teeth, trying to smile. Now we all enjoy grazing along the fence together. Why don't our humans try some of this *fence-talk*? Maybe they will take a hint from us and end these silly range wars.

Oinking at the horses

Fence-Talk

TALE 10

"A Camping We Will Go!"

In spite of the many adventures we all share down here in Pig Heaven, Mom still sometimes feels that something is missing. One day as she was driving into town, she spied what could be just the thing—a used motor-home sitting by the road with a for-sale sign in the window. An idea instantly flashed into her mind. Why not take up camping? This would be a fun way to get away for short times. Afterall, there were dozens of parks and campgrounds in our area that would be fun to visit and explore. So, she stopped and checked out the camper she had just passed.

It was old and run down, but cheap. She thought it would be just perfect, because she was planning on taking us with her and therefore didn't want something new or fancy. Also, we would only be going short distances from home. She was delighted when she looked inside. This old motorhome had a bathroom, kitchen, couch and bed, even air-conditioning. It was just like a small house on wheels. She bought it right there and then.

She originally planned to take us all camping with her, but after parking the camper in the driveway, realized that Oink would not be able to come with us. He was too big. He wouldn't even be able to walk down the center isle or to turn around, nor could anyone else if he were stuck in the middle of things. Also, he was too heavy to walk up the special boarding ramp Mom had purchased. It's capacity was 200 pounds, but Oink now weighed over 300 pounds! We all felt sad that he wouldn't be able to join us, but Mom talked Cheri into pig-sitting whenever we would be away.

Our first camping trip was a blast. The two parrots rode next to Mom in the front passenger seat, the seatbelt securely fastened around their cage. Mom had already taught them to sing "A Camping we will go, High Ho the merry-O, A camping we will go," and we all joined in as the old motor-home cruised merrily down the road. Mom had guessed it would be difficult to find campgrounds that would allow pigs, but she was happily mistaken. Most park managers thought it was a fun idea, as long as the pig was well mannered. And, of course, I was just that! Mom had already trained me to use a leash, so she would be able to take both Pepper and me for walks around the park.

Also, she had purchased a small portable fence, that folded up for easy storage. After she parked the camper, she rolled out the awning and set up the fence, which made a nice little yard for Pepper and me. Now Mom didn't have to worry about us running away or about other critters bothering us.

This setup proceedure was a bit frustrating, but once it was complete, we were right at home. Mom took Pepper and me for long walks, and the campers were delighted to meet us. They had never seen a pig camping before, so they all gathered around and asked dozens of questions. I let them pet me and give me treats. This attention never stopped. Many campers came over to our site to visit and talk about pets and camping. We discovered in these chats that most campers are pet lovers. They like to camp because they can bring their special friends with them. They really enjoyed bringing their dogs over to meet us, who were all polite and well mannered, unlike our neighbor dogs at home. They wagged their tails and made us welcome. All this attention was starting to go to my head. I was becoming one cocky little pig!

We loved playing with Mom out in our new yard, where she would sometimes lie on the ground and pretend to be taking a nap. Then Pepper and myself would nudge her and tickle her, making her flip over. Then we would go over to her other side and make her roll over again. Such a fun game, and Mom laughed and giggled.

My favorite camp activity was the campfire. Mom built ours on the other side of the fence, so that we wouldn't walk in the ashes or get burned. I would stand as close as I could get to the glowing embers, watching the sparks leap into the cold night air. The campers next door came over to roast marshmallows and listen to pig tale.

The parrots stayed inside, as Mom feared it was too cold to bring their cage outside. She placed their cage on a table in front of a big window which overlooked our yard, shaded and protected by the pull-out awning. There they watched our every move. These avian campers chattered so loudly that Mom feared they might bother the other campers, but no one seemed to notice. When we were all inside with the door shut, Mom would let them out of their cage. Then we all watched TV and shared snacks—just like home, but lot's more fun!

Time passed much too quickly, and it was soon time to pack up and return home. Mom rolled up the awning and folded up the fence, not a bad chore at all. We all waited patiently inside the camper, as we were quite tired from all the fun adventures. Everyone but Mom slept all the way home.

Well, we were all having so much fun that we barely thought about poor old Oink. Cheri came over to feed him and visit, but he was all alone at night and for most of the day. He missed us so much that he refused to come out of his house, not even to eat. Cheri coaxed and coaxed, but to no avail. He wouldn't even come out for a belly rub. He was pouting. He missed his family, but he was also feeling slighted that we had left him behind. When we pulled into the driveway, he waddled out to meet us and squealed with delight. That night he ate so much that his belly dragged the ground! Mom felt sorry for him, so she let him sleep inside with us. He let out a sigh of deep relief as he plopped down in his favorite spot in front of the fireplace!

Mom has been so upset by the distress that our absence caused Oink that she is now reluctant to leave him for long, especially over night. So, she is planning to trade the old motor-home on a bigger one so that Oink can come along too. Wow, this will surely cause a stir in the campgrounds. Can you imagine two pigs on a leash!

Mom has promised that as soon as we get our new motor-home, she will mount a custom license plate on the back, cautioning: "PIGS ON BOARD." And, another for the front bumper to declare: "PIGS RULE!"

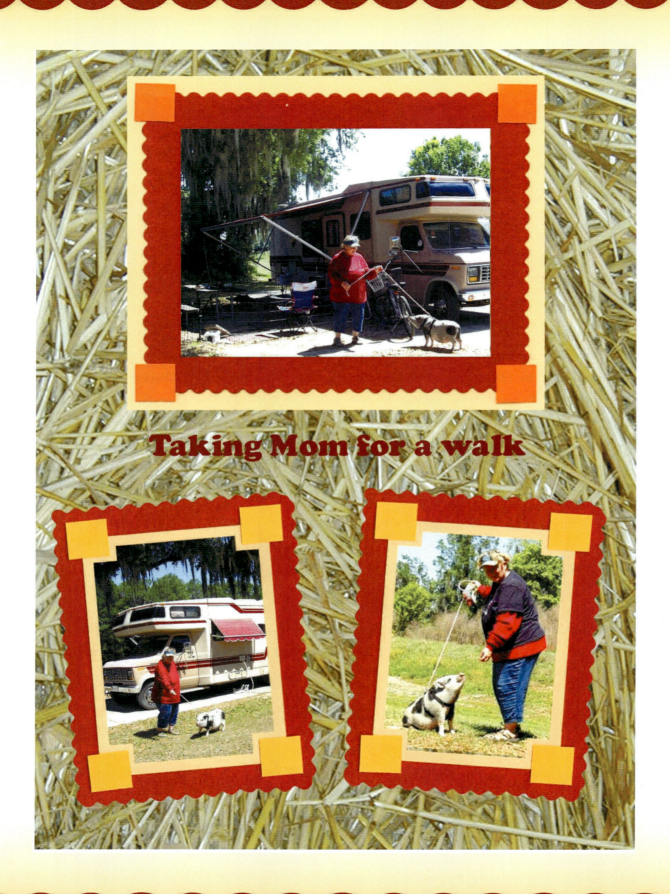

Taking Mom for a walk

How about a cold one?

Camp Games

Where's the Marshmellows?

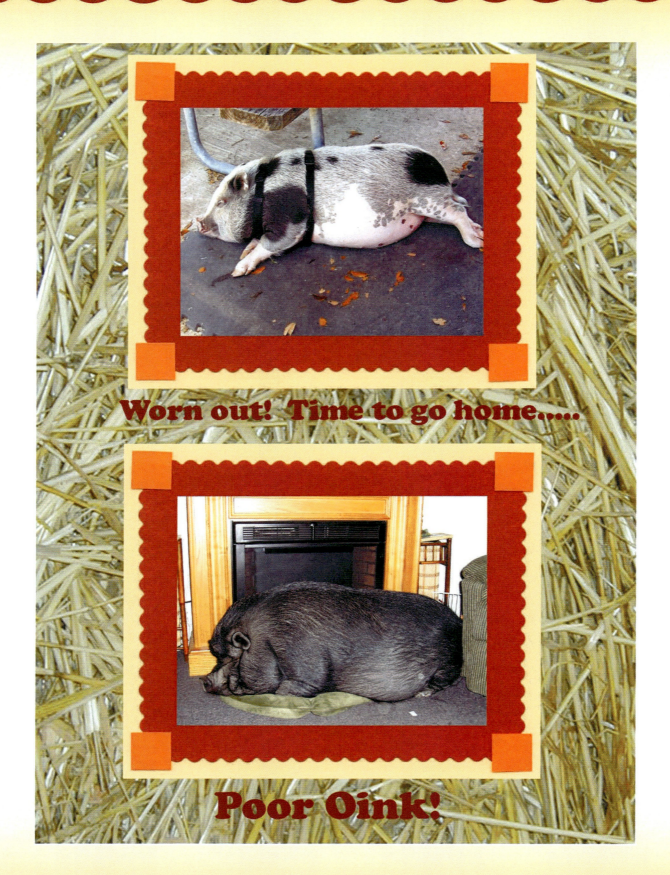

Worn out! Time to go home.....

Poor Oink!

FINAL TALE

Well, guess what? Almost a year has passed, but we still don't have our new camper. In fact, it looks like we may never go camping again, and I think I know why. There are several reasons. One is my size. I am now as big as Oink! Mom would have to have two RV's to handle us both! But, I am not the only one with an expanded waistline—just look at our Mom! She has gained so much weight that walking or standing causes much pain in her feet and legs, so she now must rely on her electric cart much more than before. Also, the cost of fuel has almost doubled, which is too much for Mom's limited budget. In fact, most things seem to be too expensive now days, making it necessary for us all to stay close to home and live a simple life style. Mom calls this a **recession**. But, we pigs don't mind, as long as we are all together here in PIG HEAVEN.

Mom, on the other hand, has once again slipped back into depression and boredom, seldom laughing at our usual antics and tricks. She seems so distant and worried, only occasionally forcing a smile. To make matters worse, she was recently forced to sell our old camper and use the money for a new roof.

On this past Valentine's Day, Mom and Cheri decided to go to a nearby flea market, hoping to find some bargains to bring home and spread some cheer. Oh no! Remember what she brought home the last time she went to the flea market? *Little old ME!*

Sure enough, Mom arrived with a new critter to add to our flock. She came upon a bird booth, and spied a baby parrot so loving and cute that she just couldn't leave without him. Thus, she dug deep into her pocket book, took out her last dollars and had the bird vendor put this tiny bundle of fluff into a cardboard box. She loved his rainbow colors with an orange and yellow head, green wings and white tummy. She decided on the way home to name him Cupid, as she found him on February 14th. About half way home, Mom peeked into the box to check on her new friend, and out he jumped, climbing up to perch on her shoulder under her big purple hat. Now Cupid could really enjoy the rest of the journey to his new home.

Well, this was a lucky day for us all. Cupid is so much fun. He plays constantly, doing tricks and getting into mischief. This little clown makes us all laugh. He doesn't talk, but sings and squawks and purrs like a cat. When Mom chats on the phone, he sits on her hand and pushes the buttons and nips her ear, sometimes squawking into the receiver and scaring the caller. Anyway, we pigs can relax a bit, as we don't have to try so hard to cheer our mom up. Cupid does a good job of that. All three of the birds' wings are clipped, so they can come outside and play with us. Mom gets out her cart, and away we go—the birds on her shoulders and Pepper and we pigs not far behind. We stop by the pond and talk to the gold fish or cruise out into the pasture to *fence-talk* with the horses. Sometimes Cupid rides on our backs. He loves to groom us, pulling on our long bristles and hairs, gently pecking off the flakes of dry skin, or rummaging around for hidden treasures such as leaves, cedar needles, blades of grasses and tiny twigs. S.B. and B.B. just sit and watch in amazement. They are still scared silly of Oink, so they screech and scream in terror when he comes near. They love to chant "Stupid Cupid" or "Cupid's Stupid!" This always makes Mom laugh, especially when this tiny comedian balances on one foot while riding upon our backs, or hangs upside down from the cart basket.

Now days Mom is seldom worried or sad. She is just too busy taking care of all of us. Besides, one or another of us always does something to make her smile. She no longer feels that something is missing or yearns to venture to far away places, and she has recently started a new diet and vows to get back into shape. She has even installed a new pink pig mailbox, although I wonder if she may be colorblind? But Mom says the color pink is a happy color, which shows everyone that our home is a happy homestead where *pigs rule*. It seems that our Mom has finally realized, like us, that everything that really matters is right here in *Pig Heaven*. Yes, indeed, life is good "*Way down upon the Suwannee River…That's where I roam….That's where I call my home.*"

February 14th will always be our lucky day!

Coming
And....

Going

Look Ma...
One foot!!!

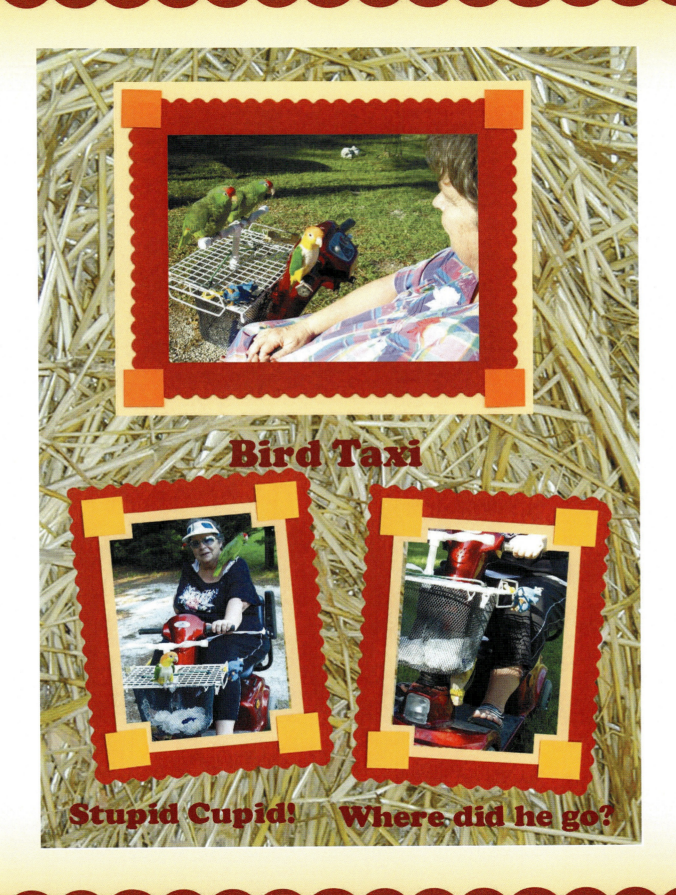

Bird Taxi

Stupid Cupid!   **Where did he go?**

Mom's pink-pig mailbox

Life is good here in Pig-Heaven!

Printed in the United States
By Bookmasters